Drawing The Ultimate Villain: The Joker

How To Draw Everyone's Favorite Villain: The Joker

How to Draw the Joker

By : Gala Publication

2

Published By :

Gala Publication
© Copyright 2015 – Gala Publication

ISBN-13: **978-1522801078**
ISBN-10: **1522801073**

Table of Contents

EASY JOKER

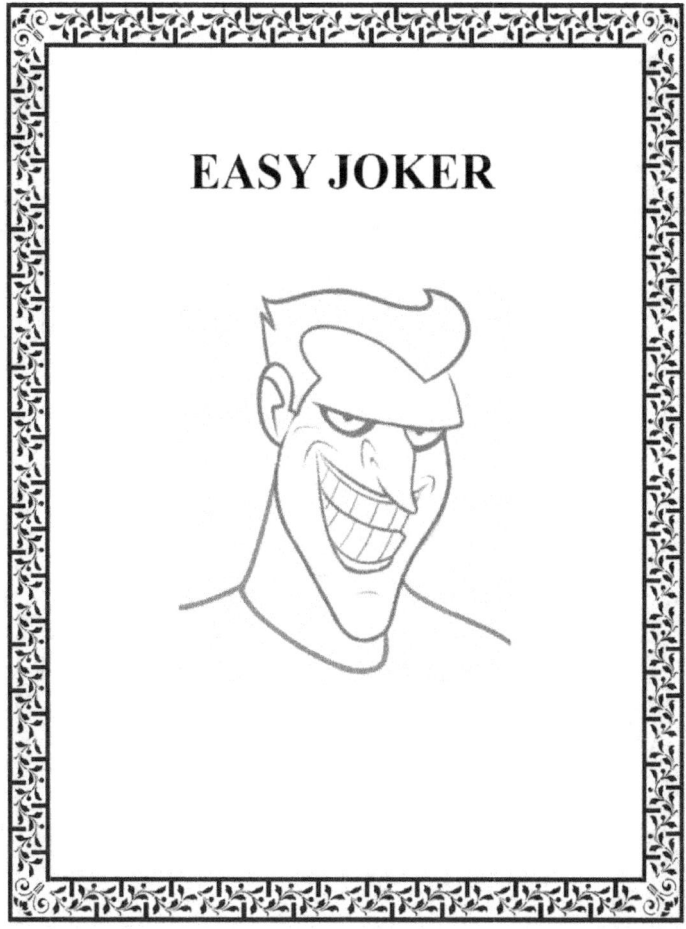

STEP 1

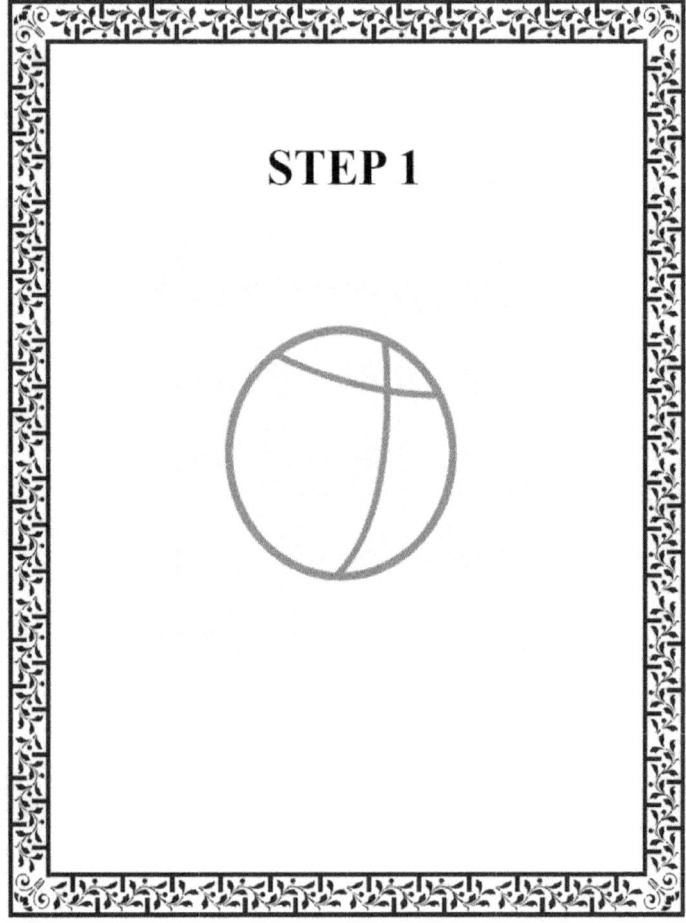

STEP 2

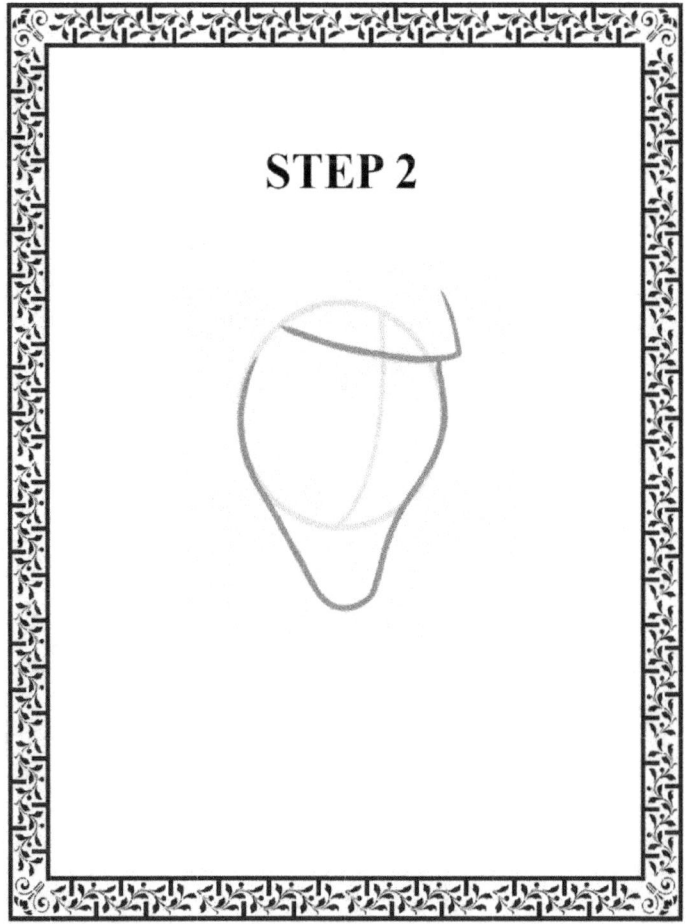

STEP 3

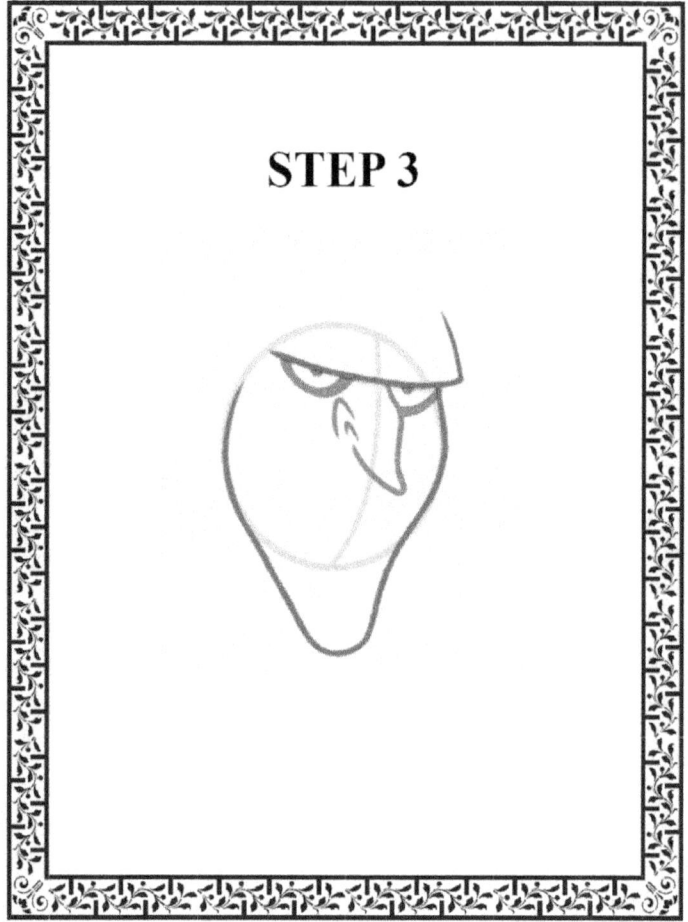

STEP 4

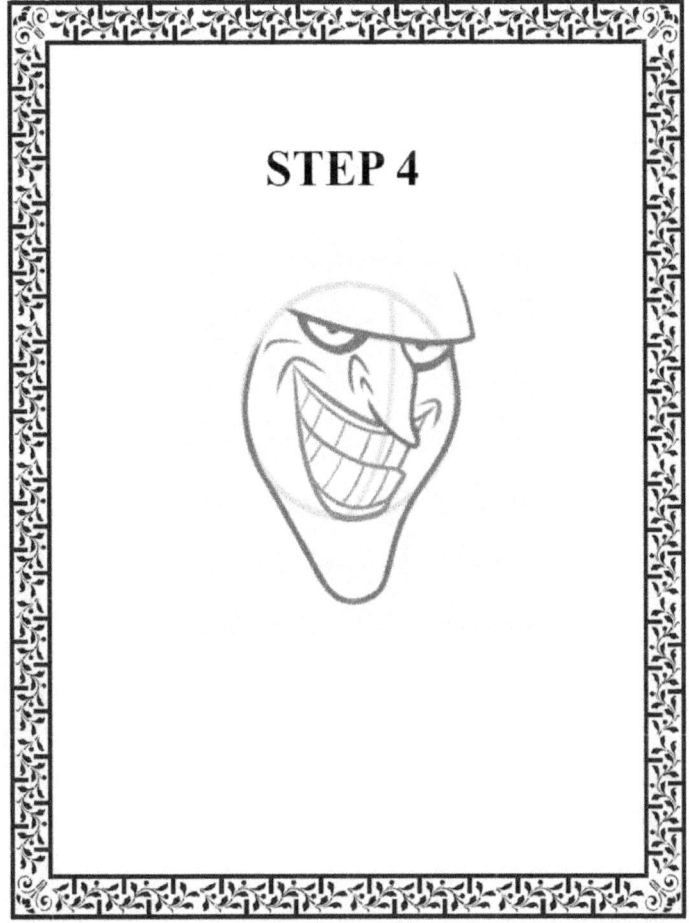

STEP 5

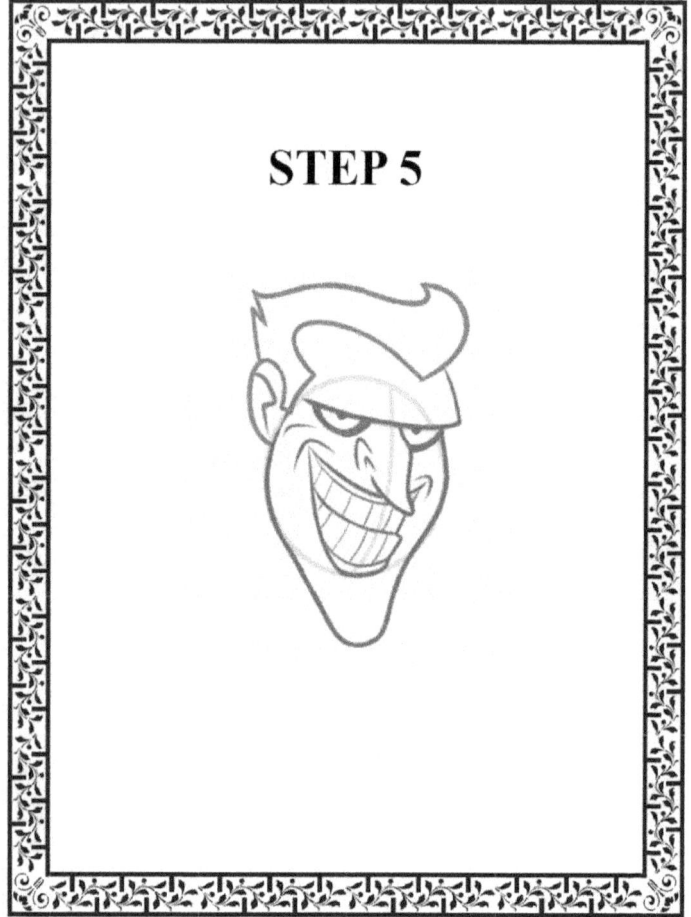

STEP 6

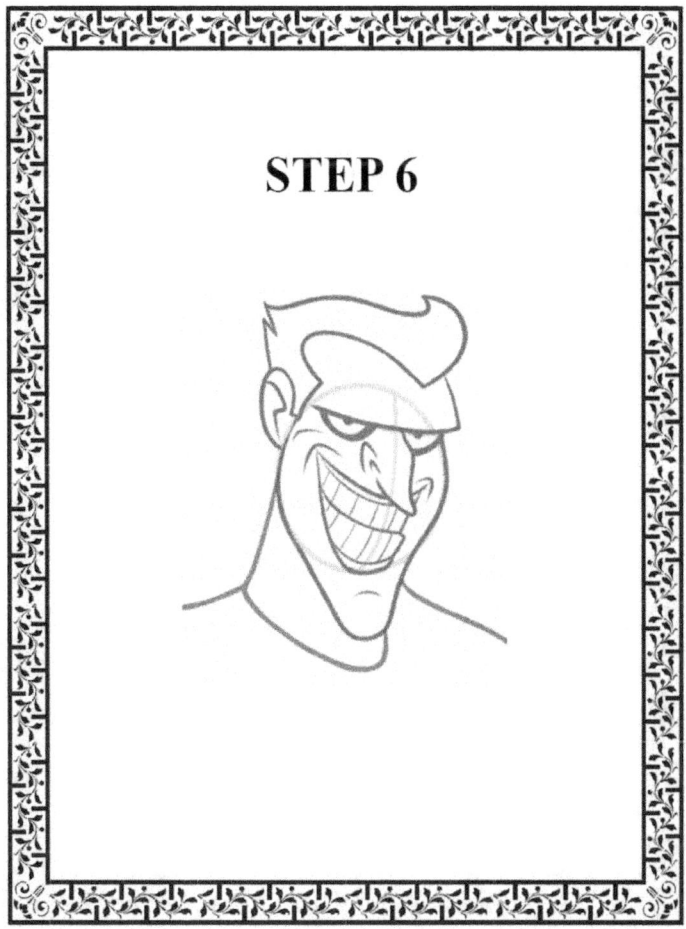

STEP 7

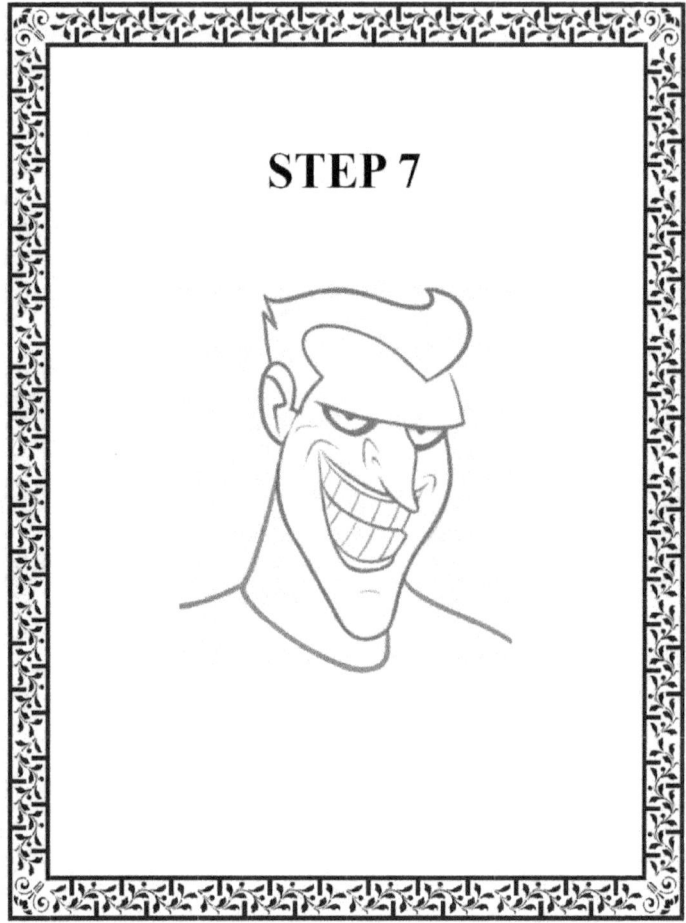

INSANE JOKER

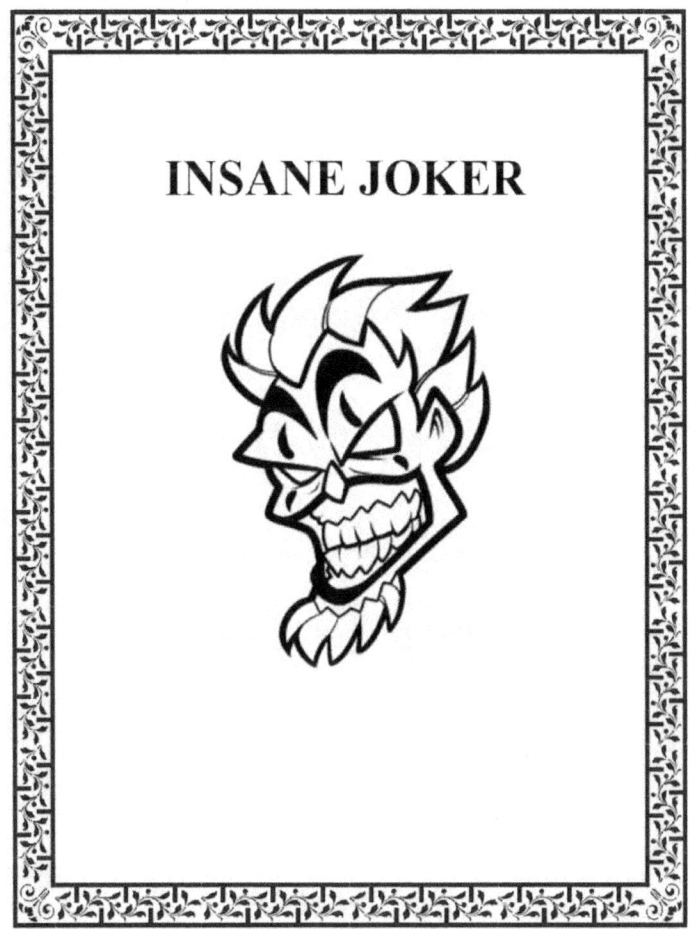

STEP 1

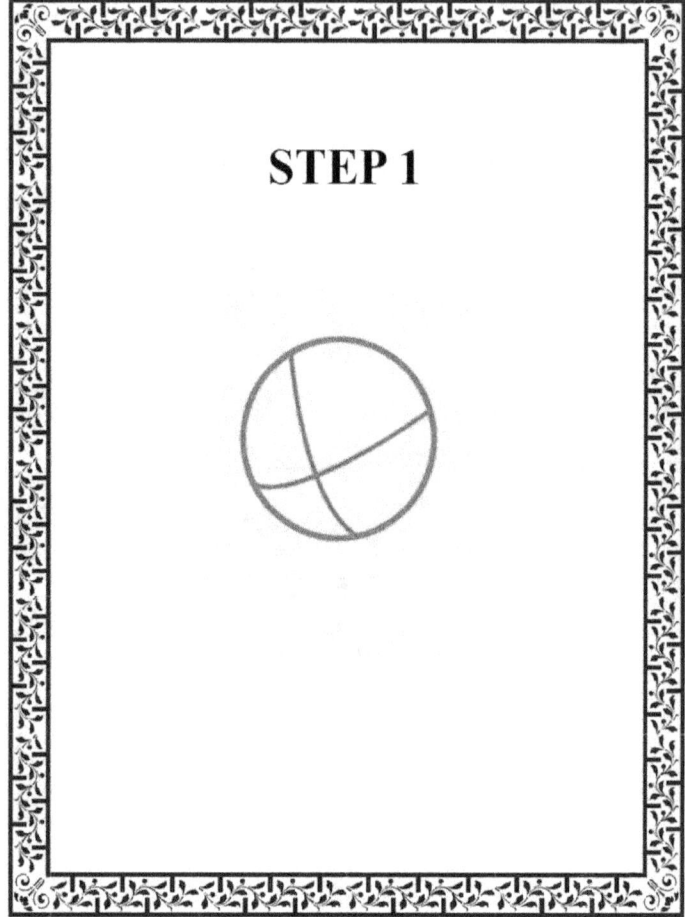

15

STEP 2

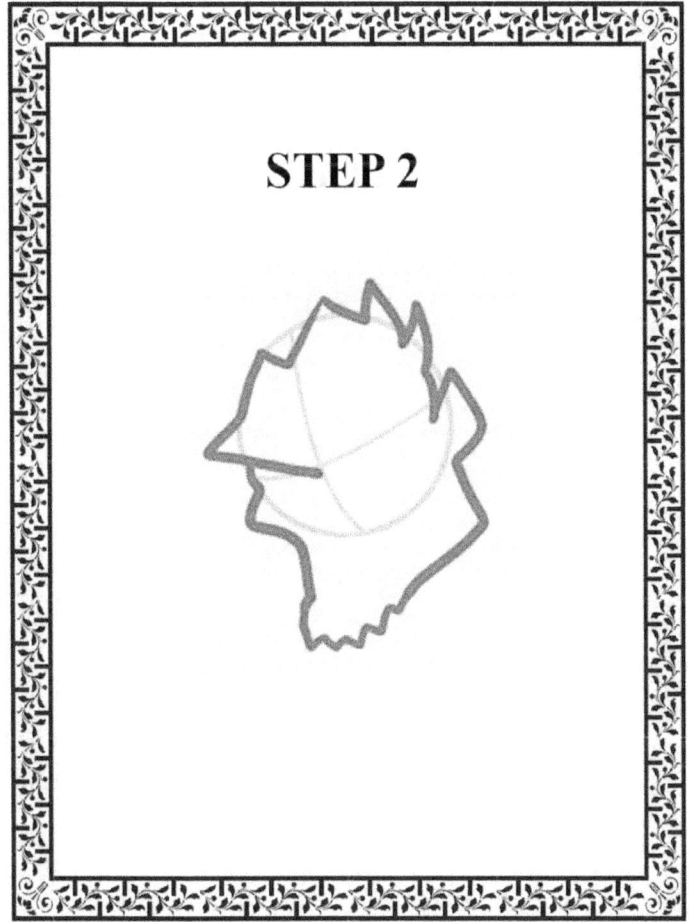

STEP 3

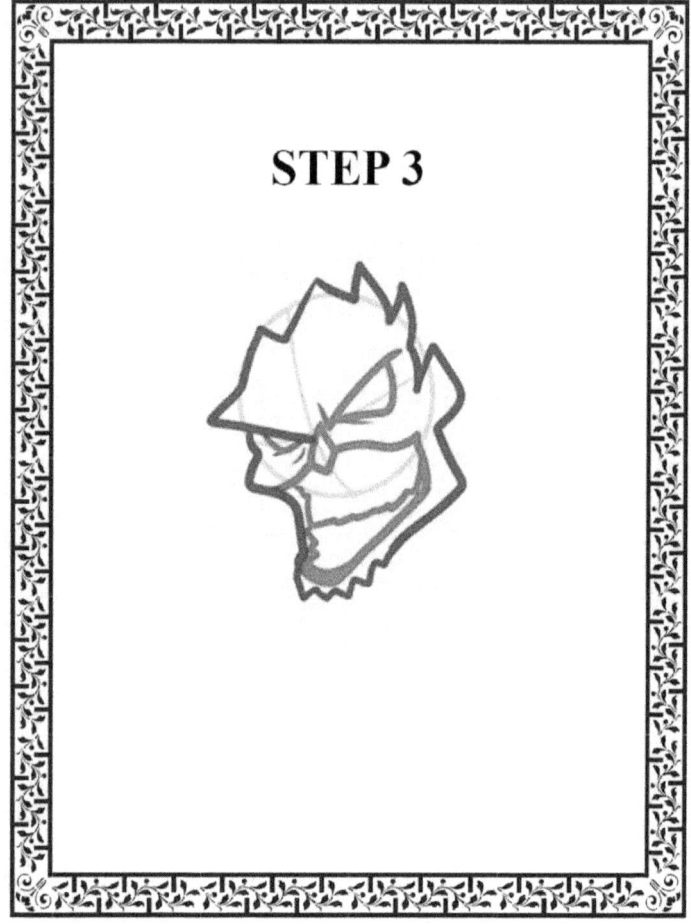

STEP 4

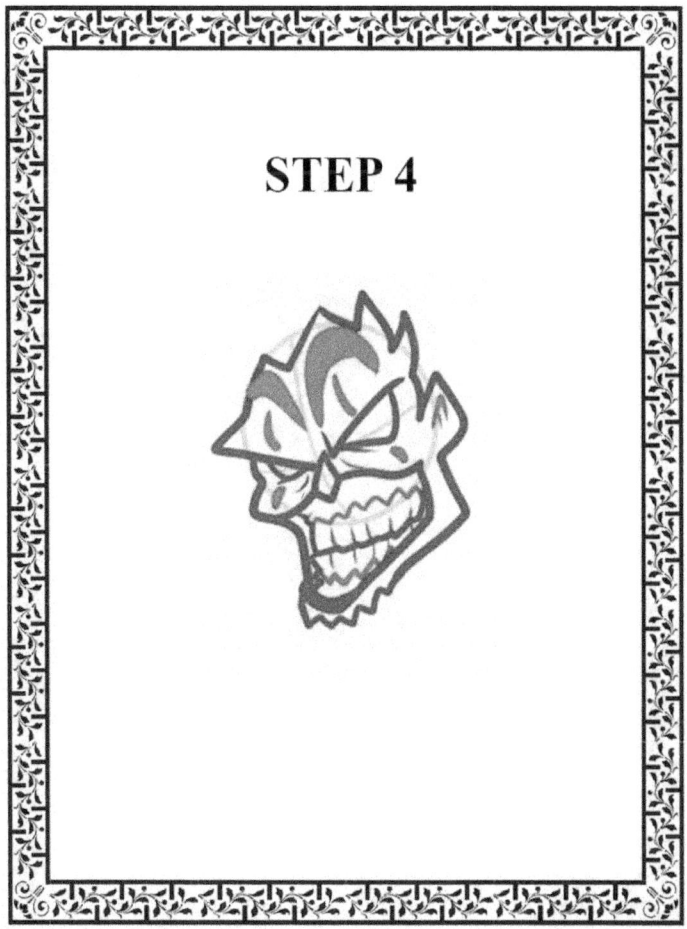

STEP 5

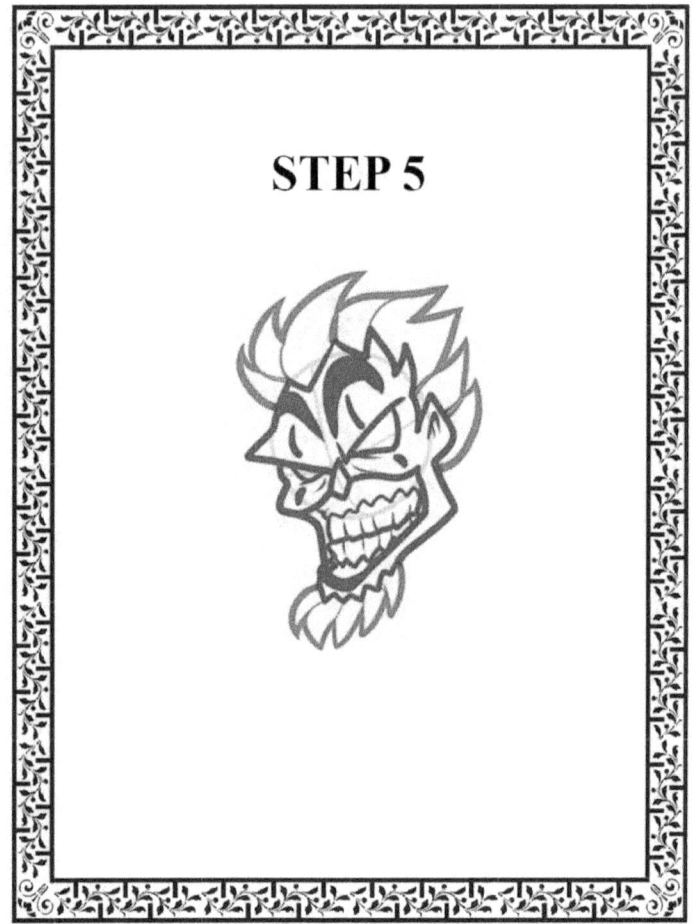

STEP 6

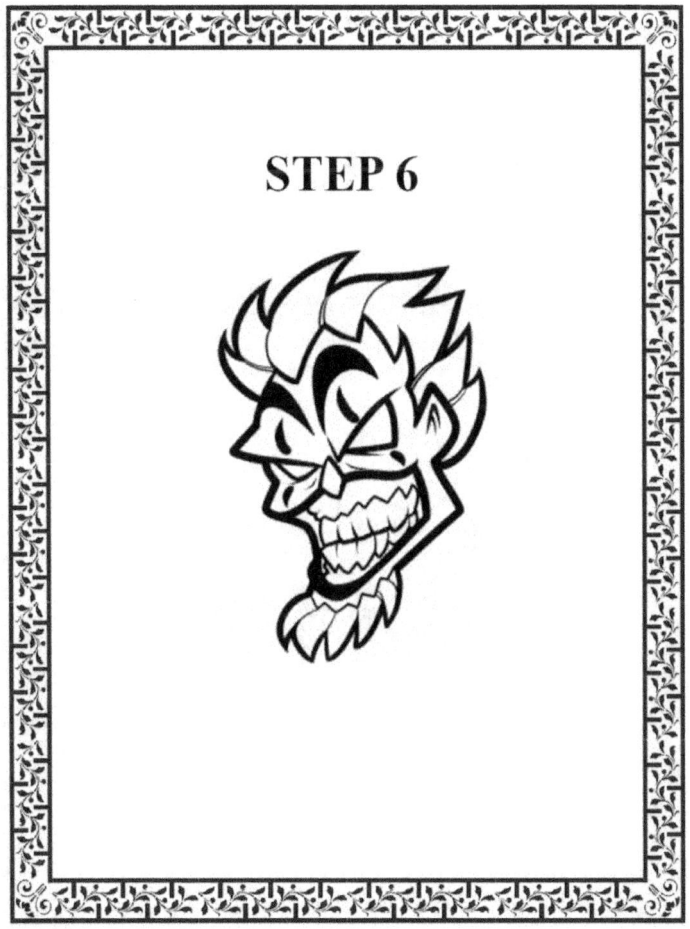

KILLER JOKER

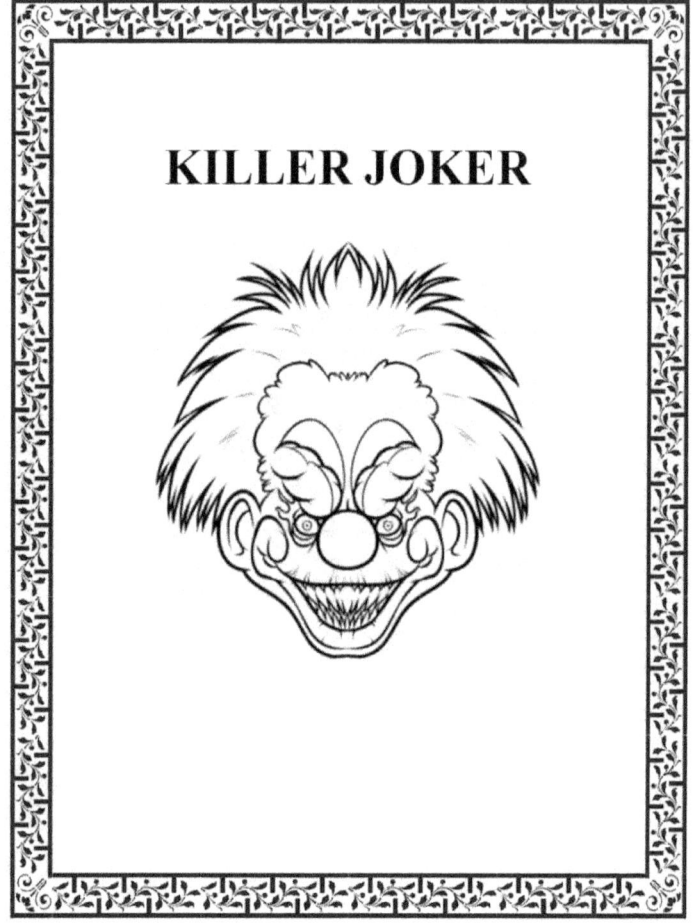

STEP 1

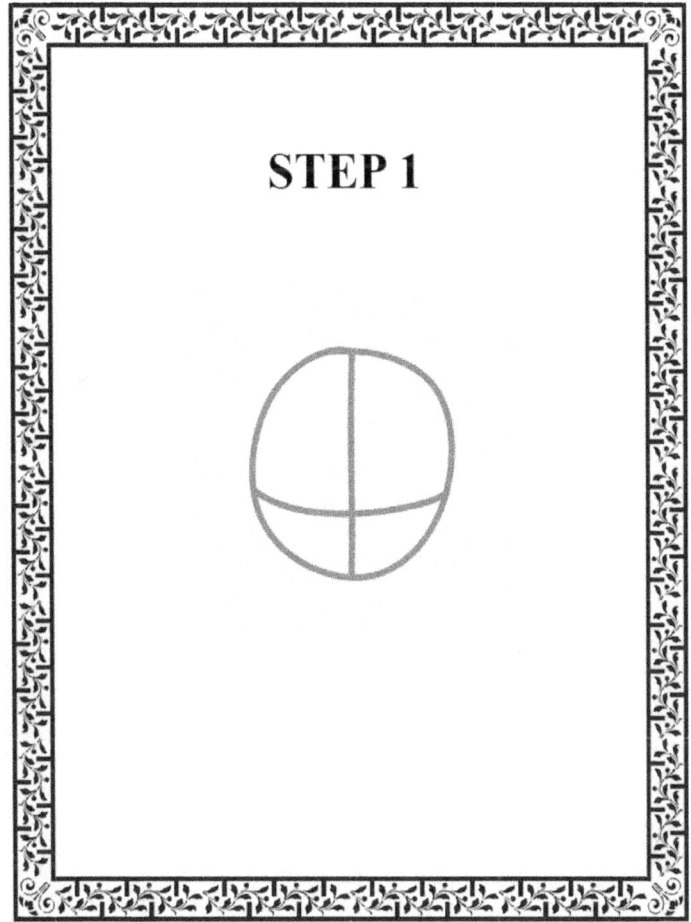

STEP 2

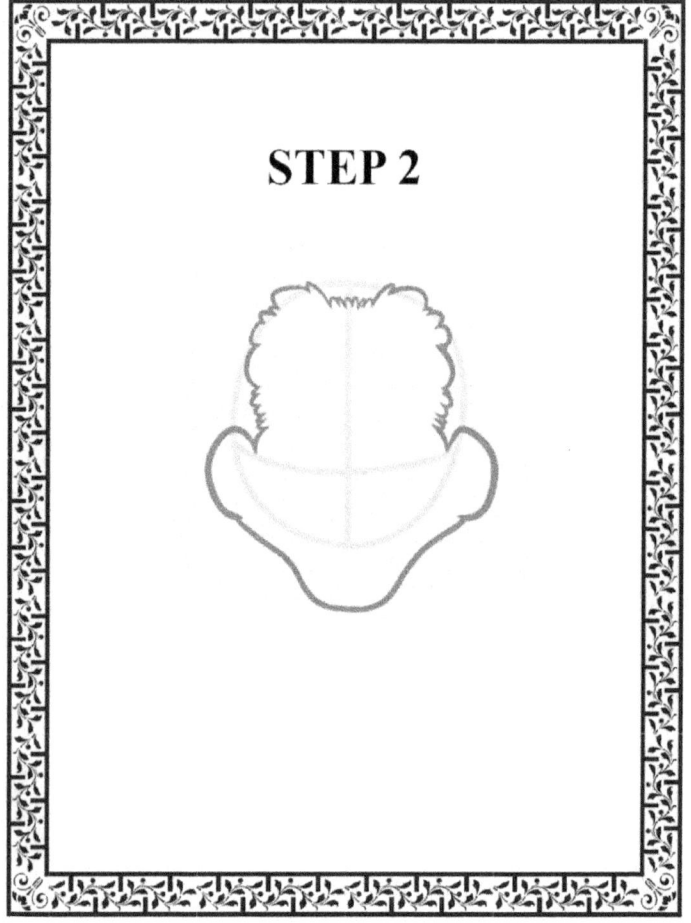

STEP 3

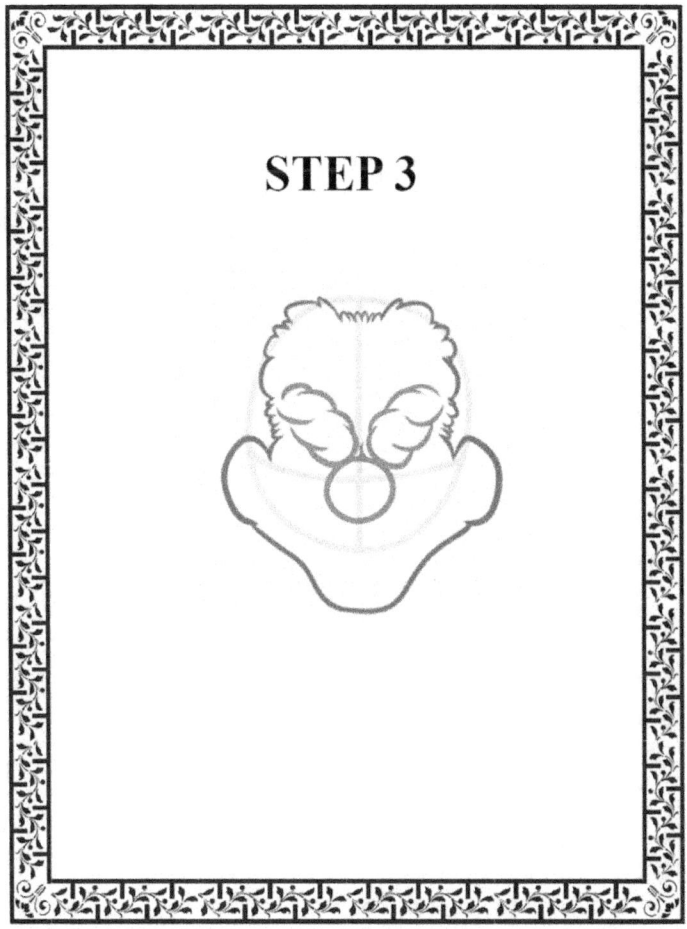

STEP 4

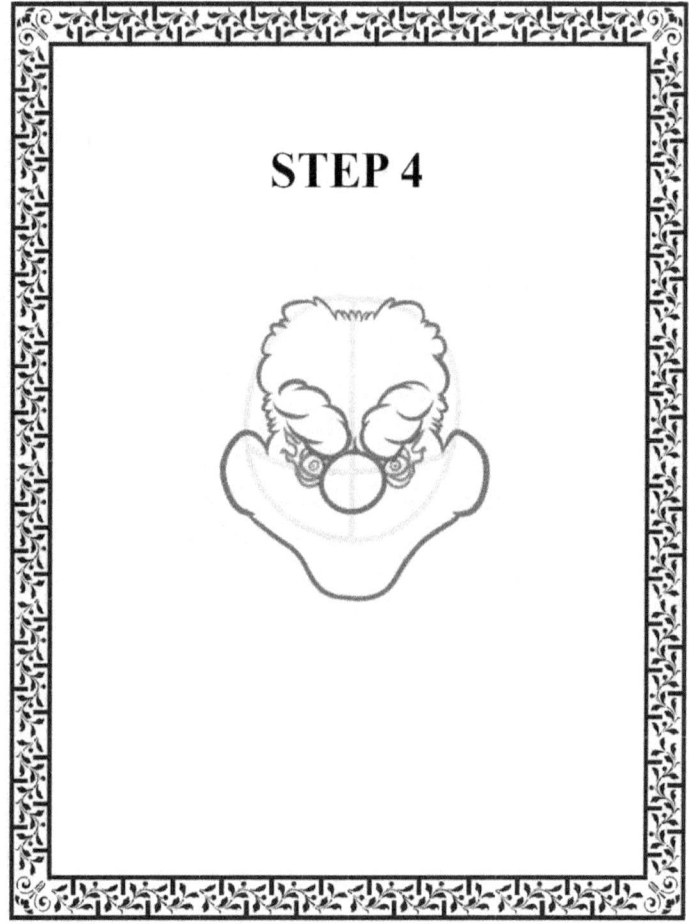

25

STEP 5

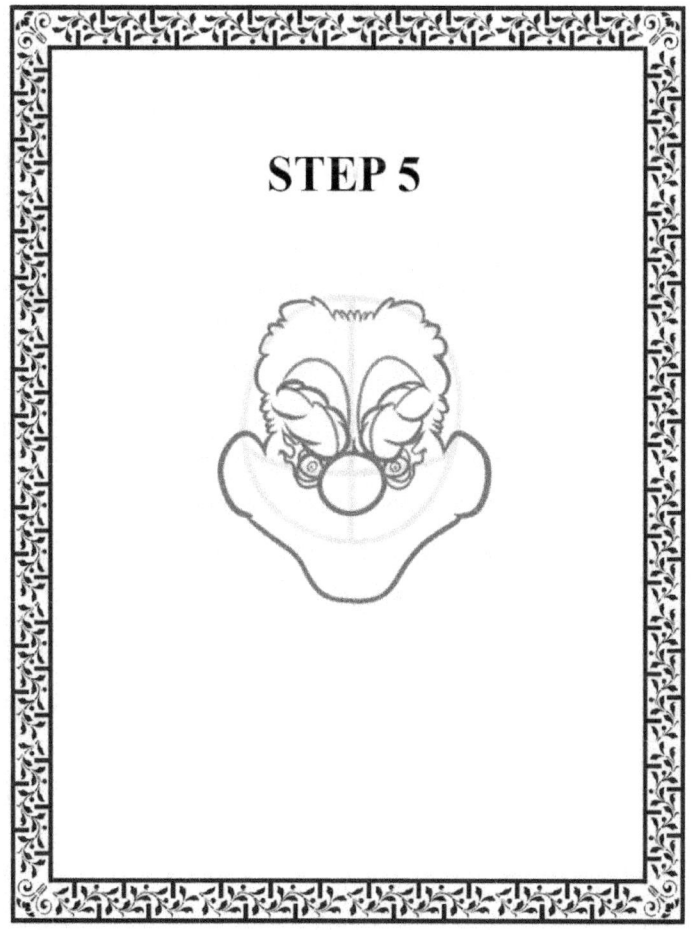

STEP 6

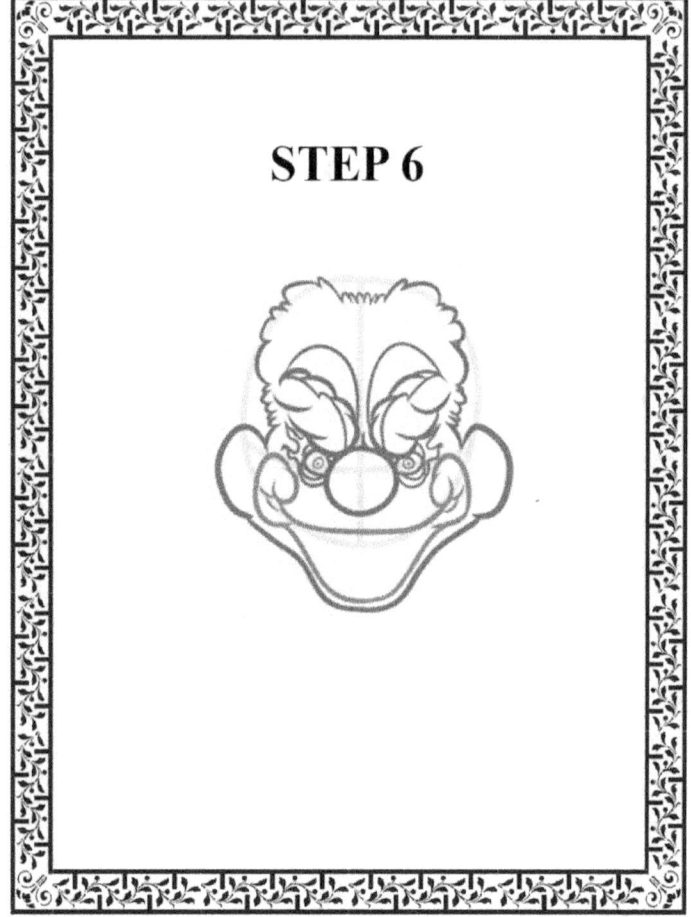

STEP 7

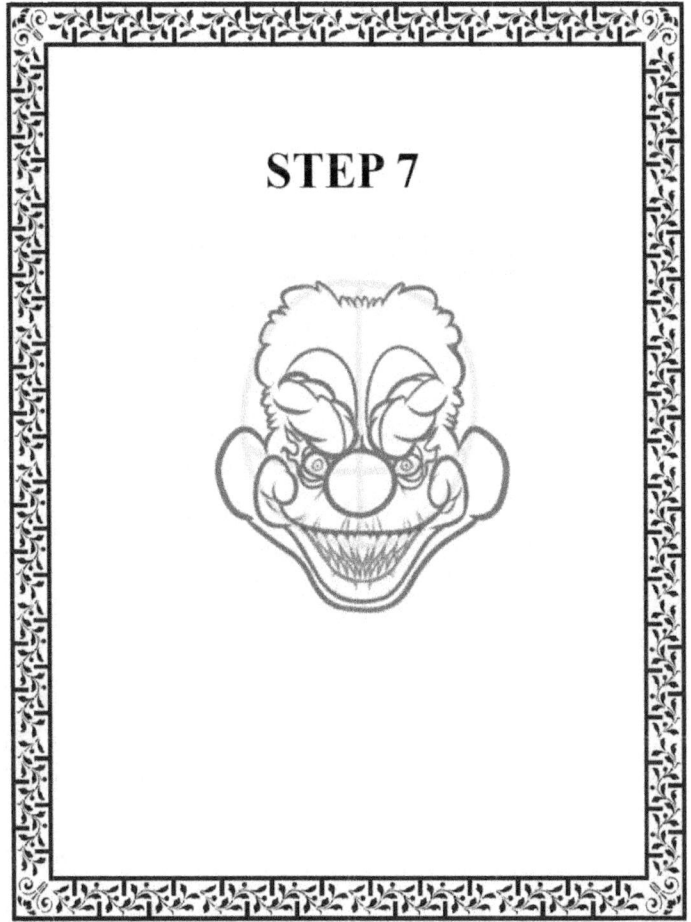

STEP 8

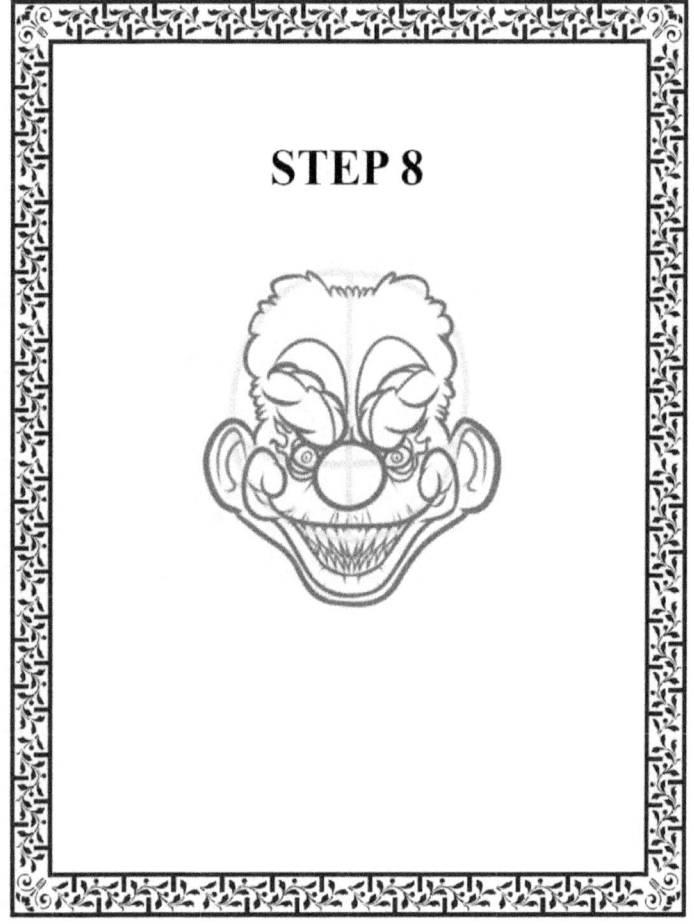

STEP 9

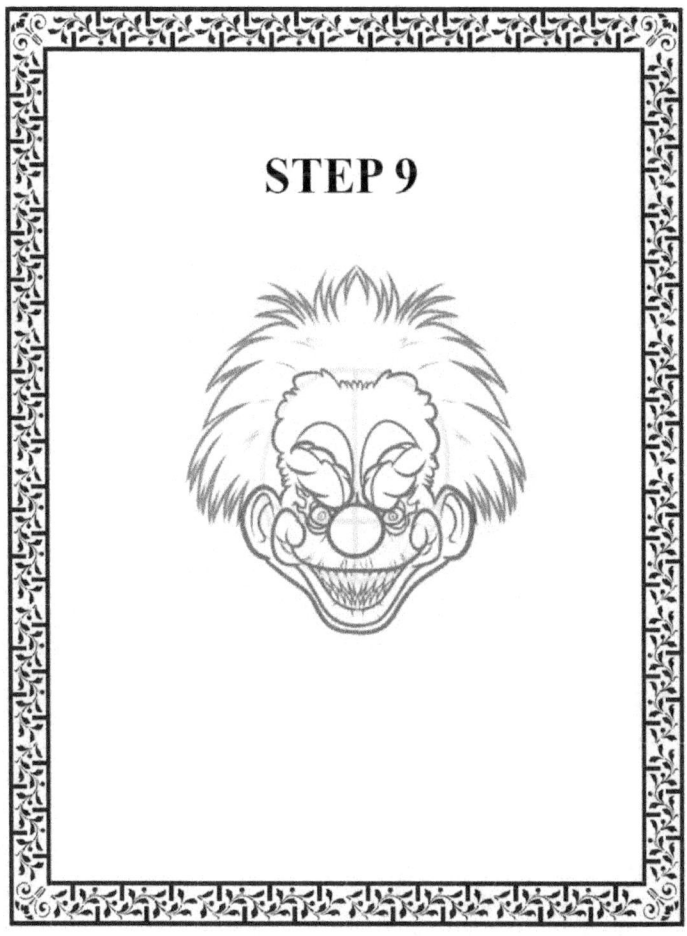

STEP 10

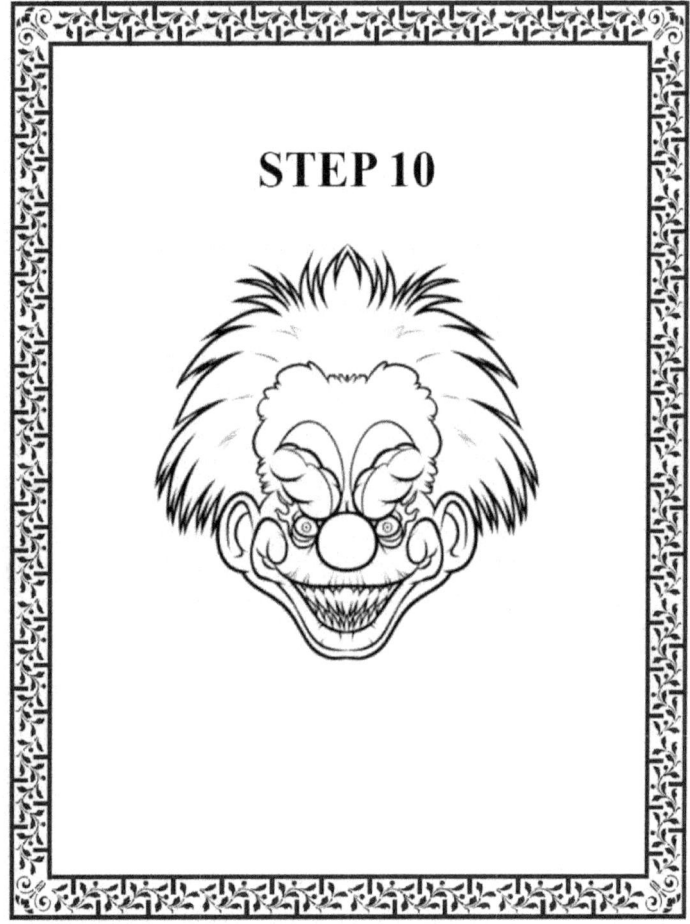

SCARY JOKER

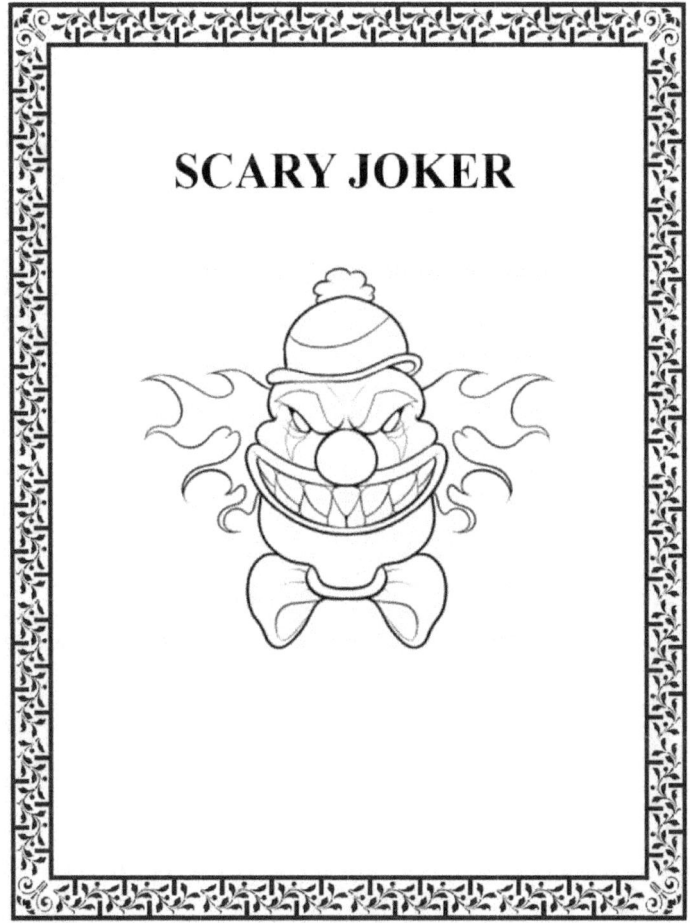

STEP 1

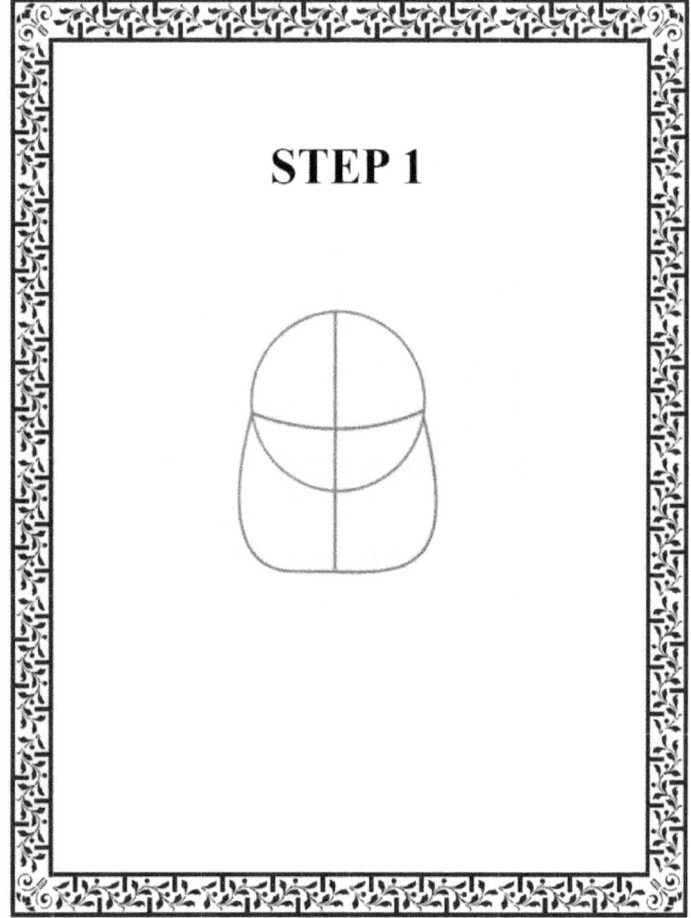

STEP 2

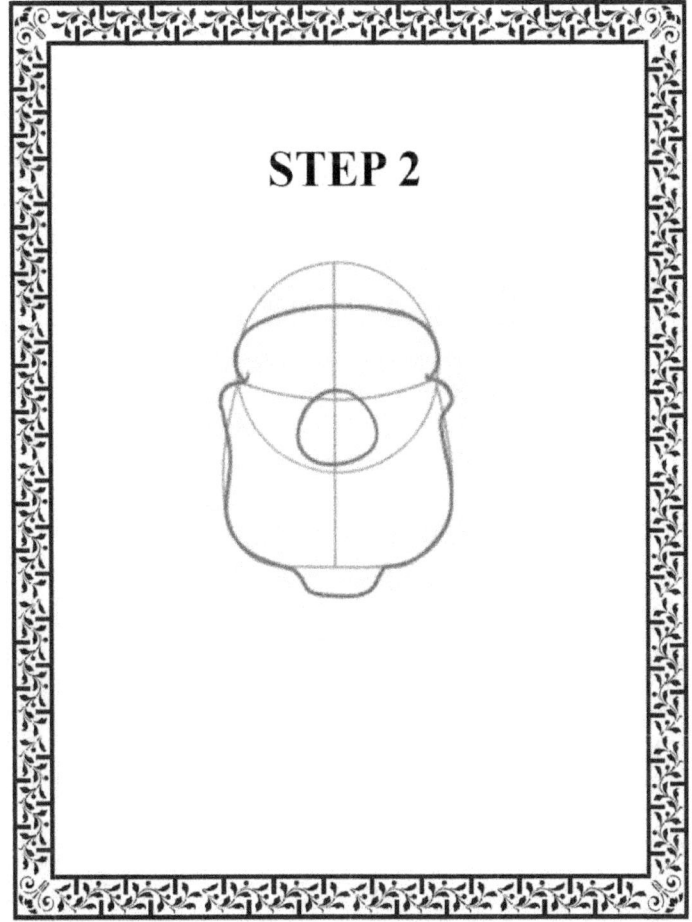

34

STEP 3

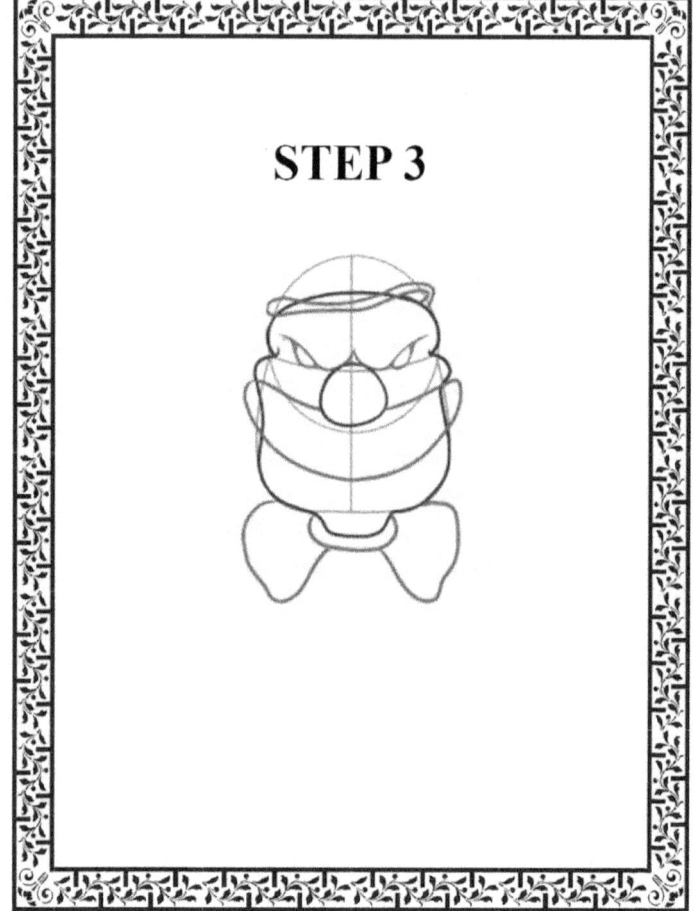

35

STEP 4

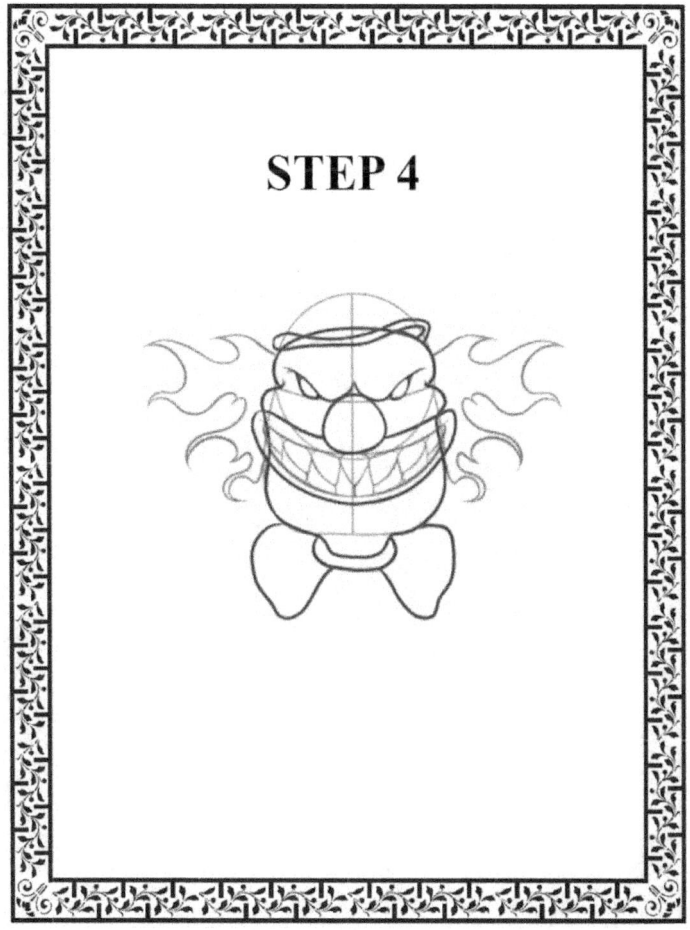

STEP 5

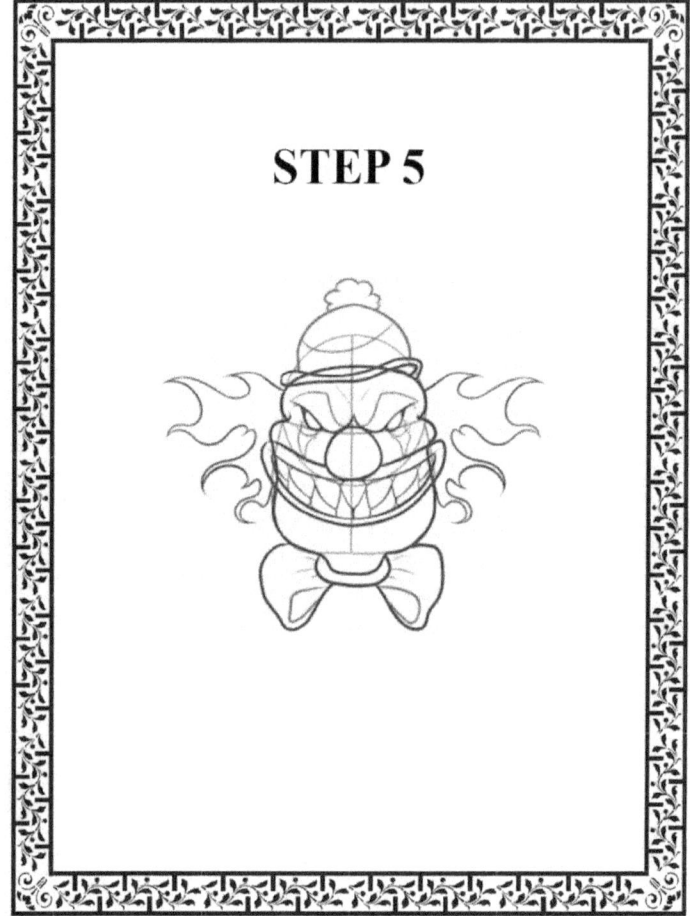

STEP 6

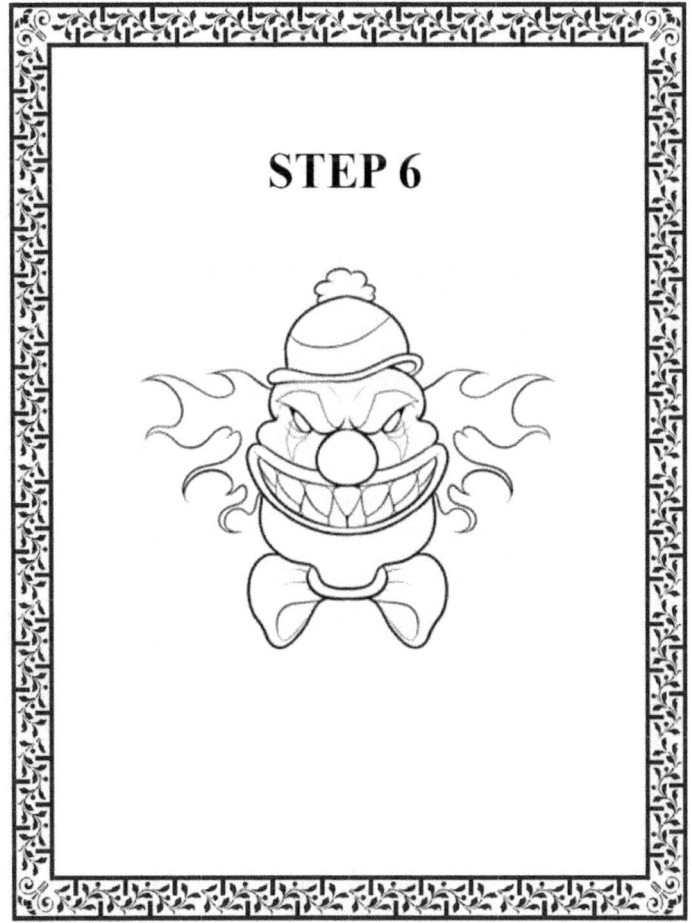

SIMPLE JOKER

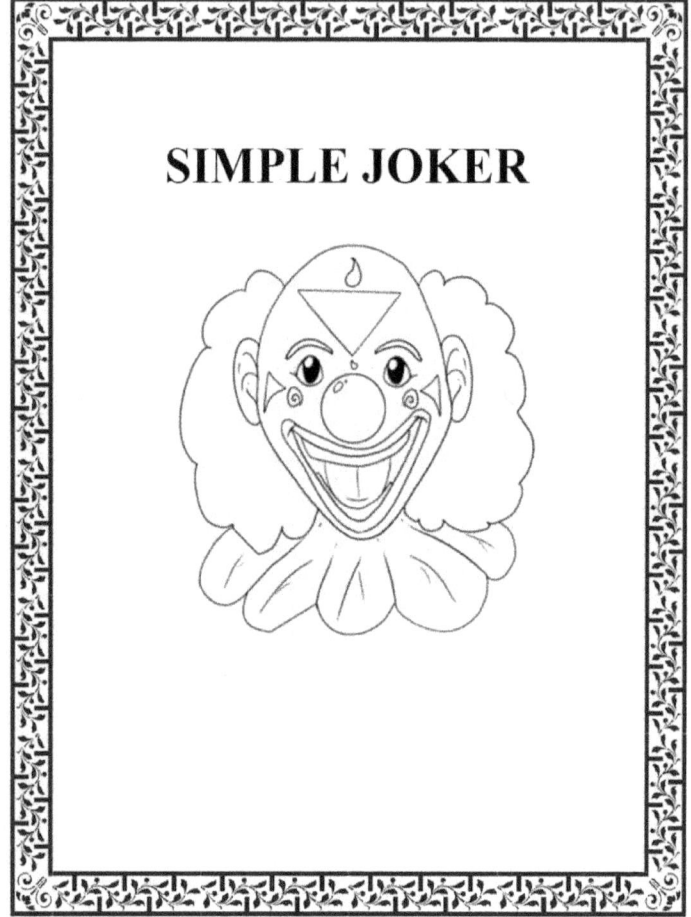

STEP 1

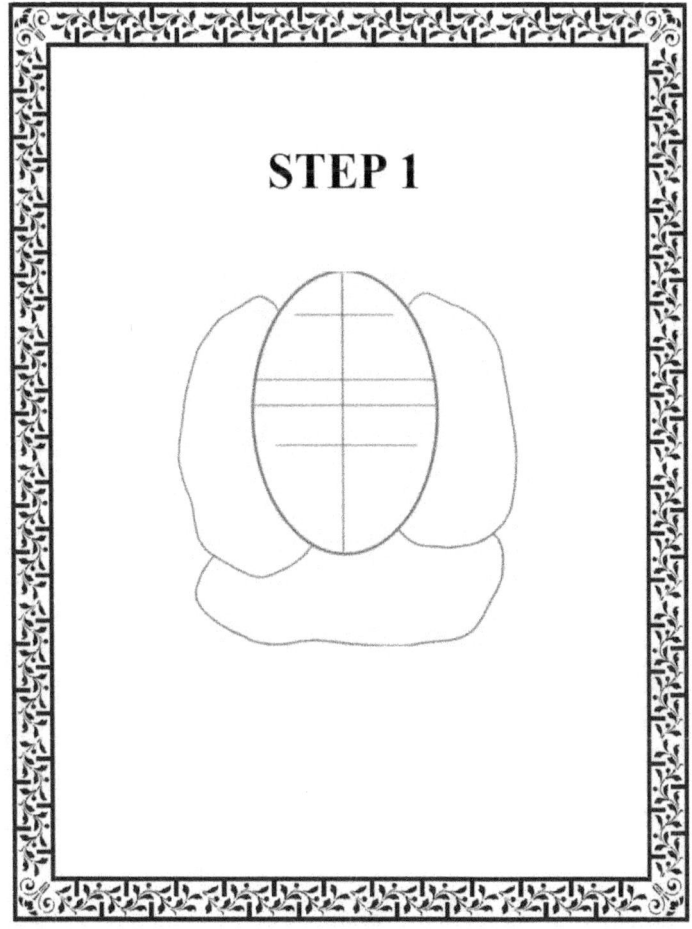

STEP 2

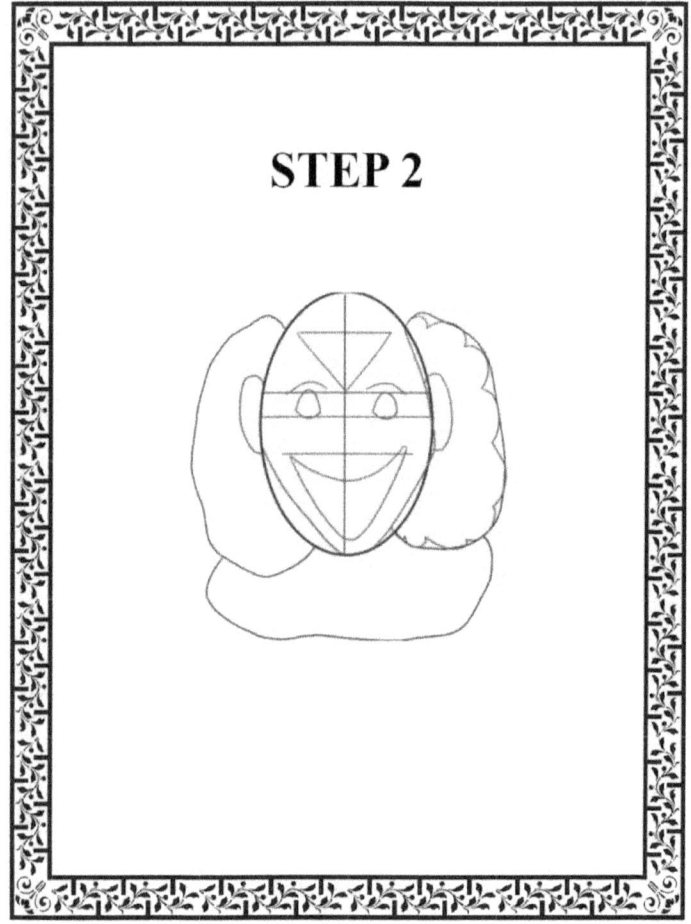

STEP 3

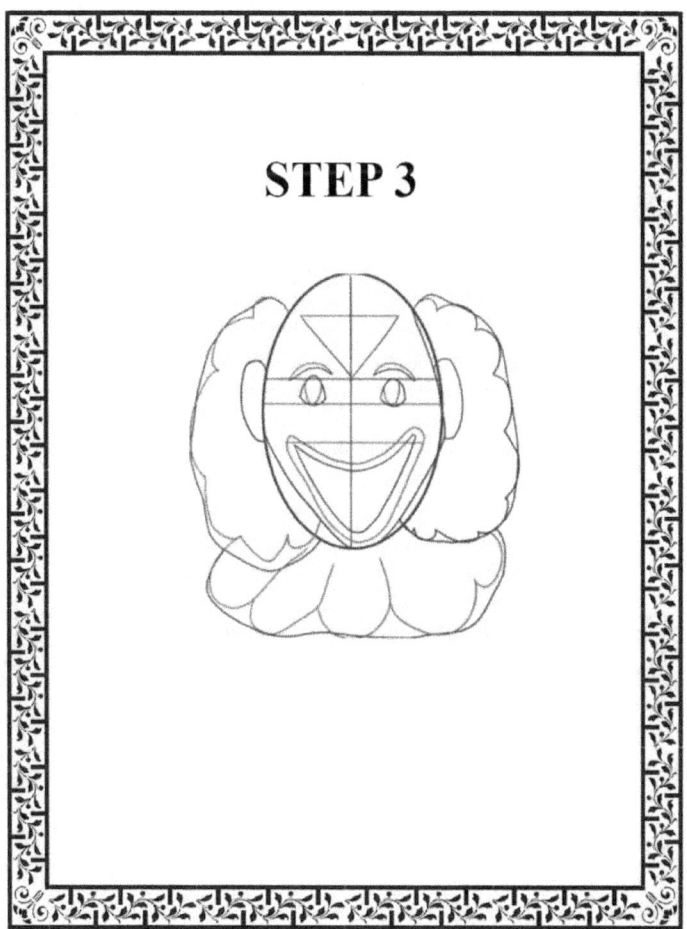

STEP 4

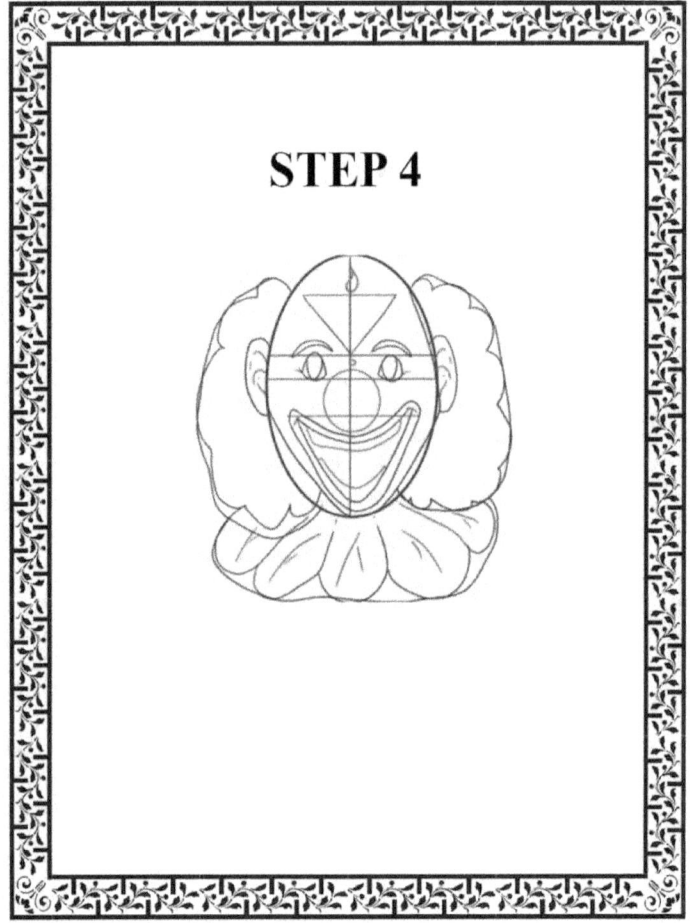

STEP 5

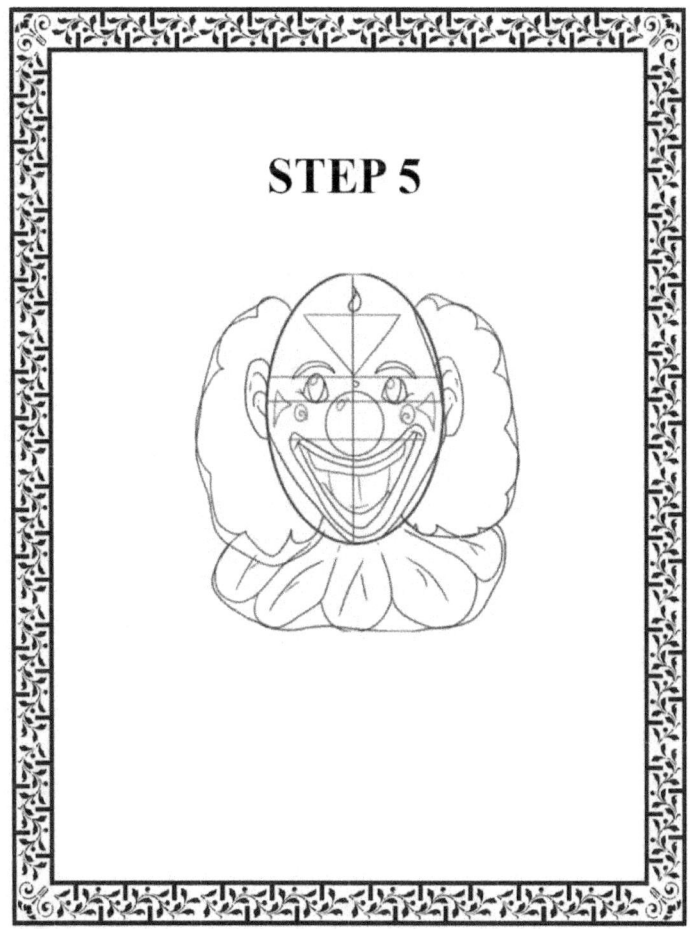

STEP 6

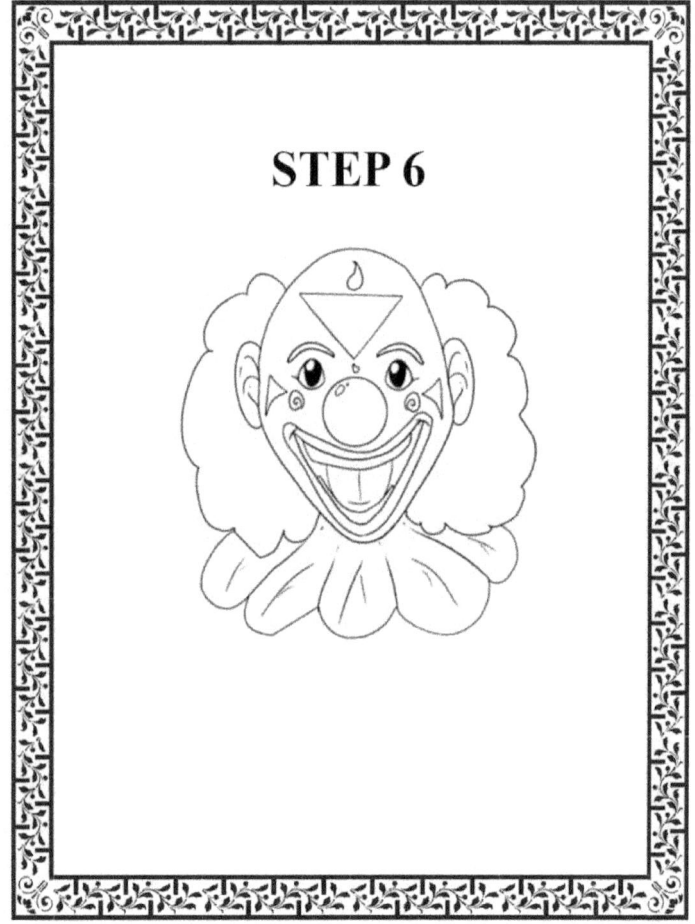

TRIBAL JOKER

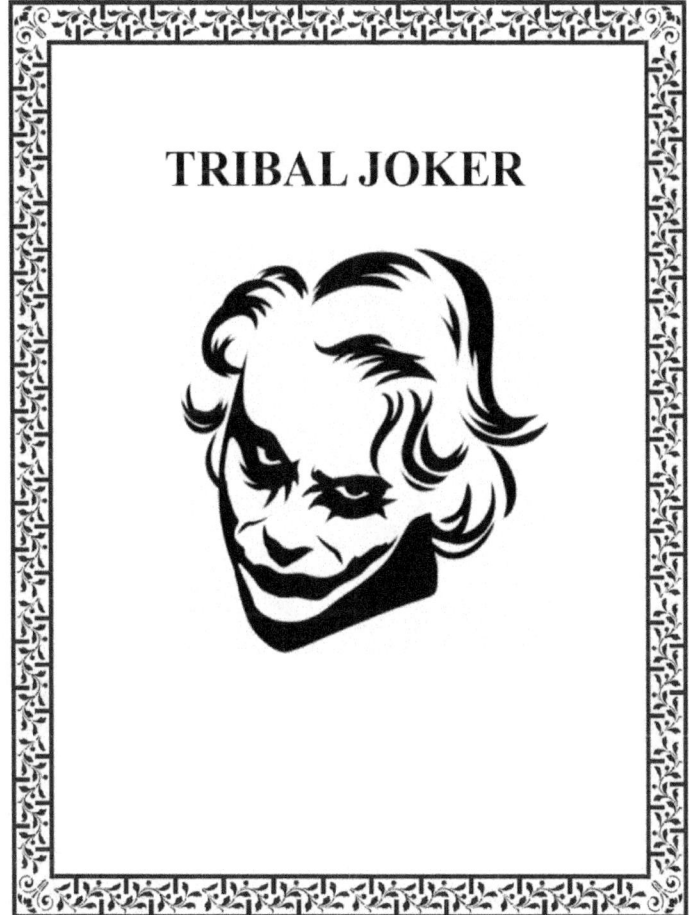

STEP 1

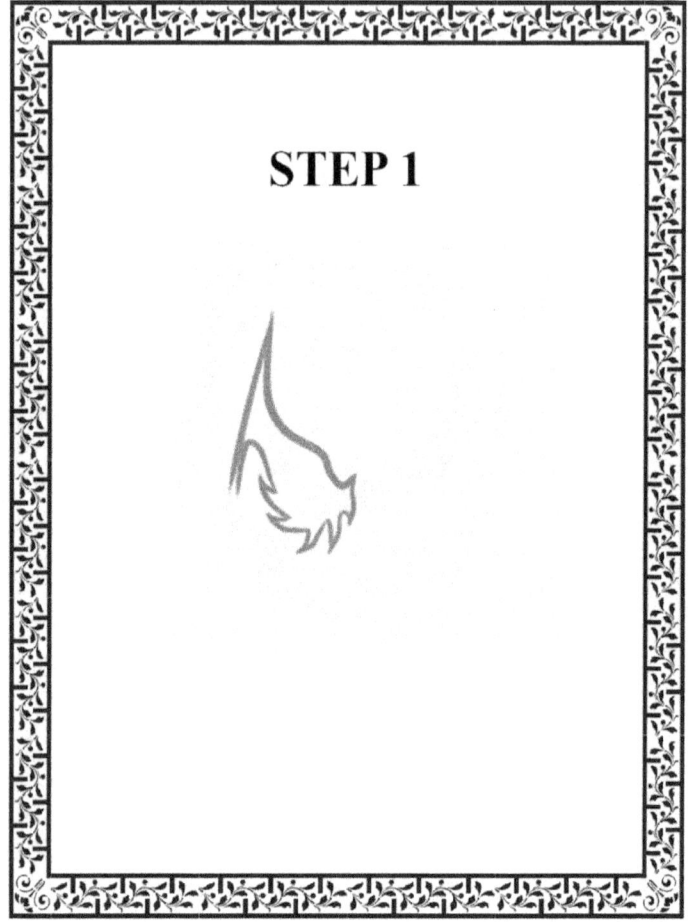

STEP 2

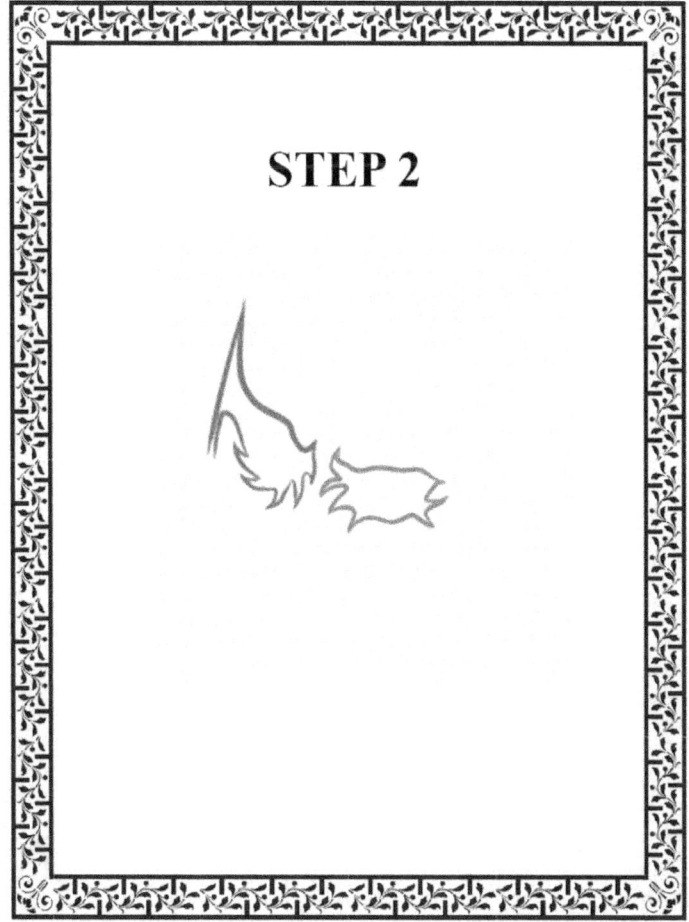

STEP 3

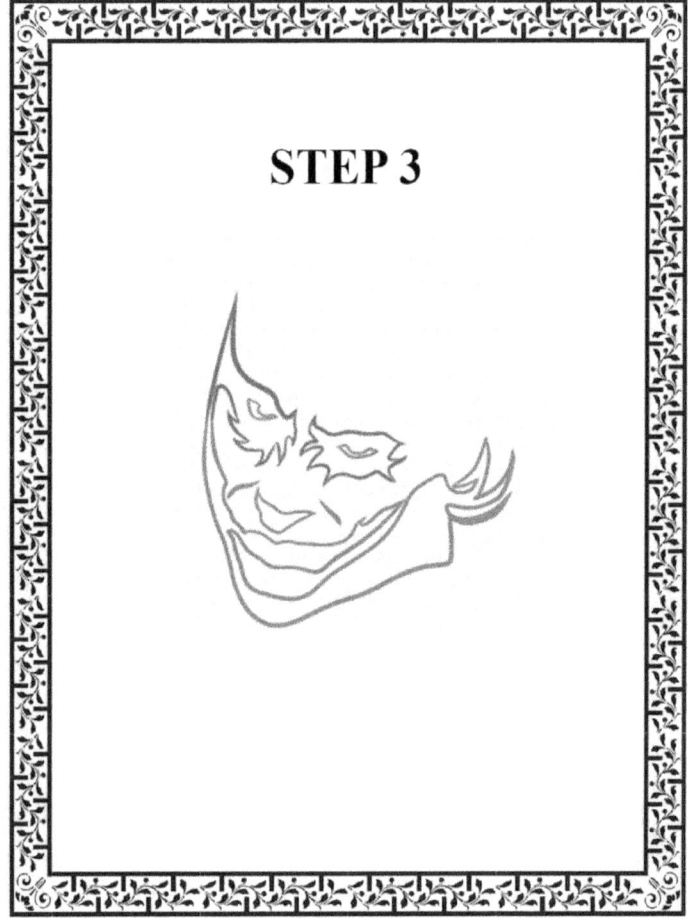

STEP 4

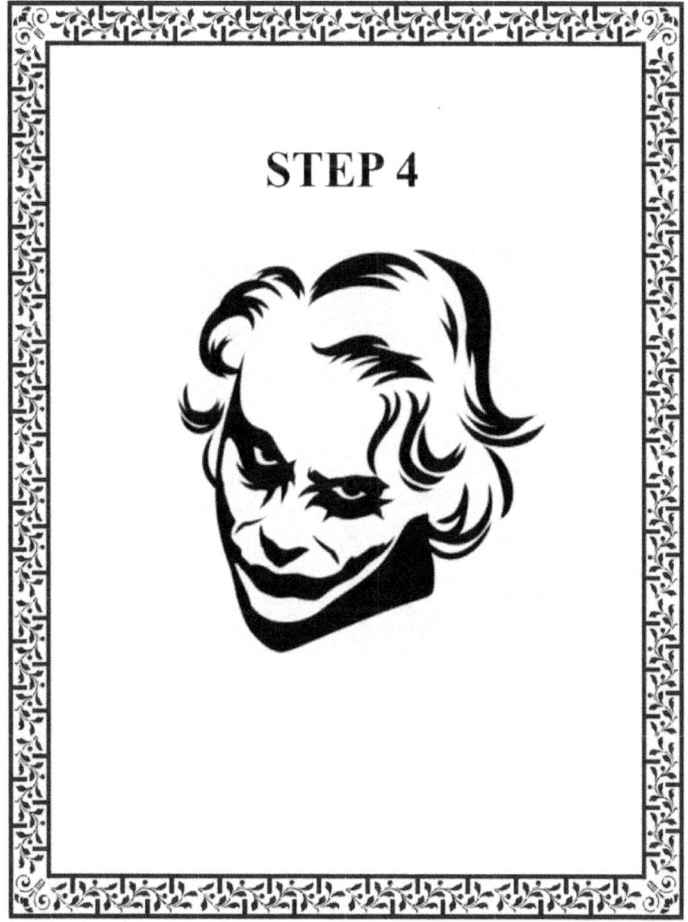